The Echo Within Us

Reflections on Life, Loss, and Becoming

Neha Singh

BookLeaf Publishing

India | USA | UK

Made with ❤ on the BookLeaf Publishing Platform
www.bookleafpub.in
www.bookleafpub.com

Dedication

To the dreamers—
who see with closed eyes,
believe in the quiet,
and turn doubt into magic.
This is for you.

Preface

Acknowledgements

I want to thank everyone who kept me going, inspired me, and reminded me to keep writing—even on the days it felt hard.

To all the teachers who encouraged me, the writers whose words moved me, and the readers who made me believe that what I write matters.

1. Enigma

Sometimes my mind wants to delve
into the unknown of all the known,
to unravel the mysteries hidden
deep inside every cornerstone.

Find the dark truth never seen
or even heard by any entity,
enlighten the mankind, that
there is no bigger enigma
than their own complexity.

Yet, the deeper I go, the more I see,
that some truths are meant to stay untold.
For in the maze of endless questions,
not every answer needs to unfold.

2. Stars

We look at the stars
as if they hold the key—
to our thoughts,
the answers to our questions,
the hope in our despair,
the light in our darkness.

In their shimmer, we find
whispers of yesterday,
each twinkle a quiet promise,
reminding us there is more
than what our eyes can see.

3. Where Are We Even Going?

Everything
feels so exhausting—
like we are all
running a marathon
we never signed up for.

Each day begins
with a race against time,
chasing to-do lists,
deadlines,
versions of ourselves
we're not even sure we chose.

We run,
faster and harder,
but still feel
like we're falling behind.

Behind someone else's success.

Behind our own expectations.
Behind the peace
we thought we'd have by now.

Some days,
we forget why we started.
Other days,
we wonder if stopping
would mean failing.

But maybe
we were never meant to win this race.
Maybe
we just need to slow down,
breathe,
and remind ourselves—
we're not alone
on this tired path.

Even if the world
keeps running,
sometimes it's okay
to just walk.

4. The Time Traveller

We are a generation of distracted minds.
Overwhelmed by choices,
guided by hope,
trapped by impossible expectations.

We begin one task,
but our minds are already elsewhere.
We have forgotten how to be here.
We do many things at once,
but lose meaning in the process.

We are always trying to reach another time —
a better one,
a past we miss,
a future we haven't lived.

We tell ourselves we're moving forward,
but often,
we are only turning around.

Looking back.
Again and again.

5. Dreams

Amidst the war of the emotions
and cages of the mind,
Some dreams were stolen
So we left them behind.
They drifted far
on winds unknown,
like shattered stars
no longer ours,
slipping through
the cracks of time,
too fragile to hold,
too distant to chase.
But even in loss,
something lingers—
a quiet ache,
a whisper of
what could have been.

But we do not wait for
stolen dreams to return;

we gather what remains,
we learn to dream again.

6. Memories

The burden of our memories,
of our moments—
Shadows of our past,
scattered to the ground,
burnt ashes
of wings
destroyed by
your shallow lies,
spoken to silence
The real truth.

Our broken oaths,
shoving us forward
like a phantom hand
between our shoulder blades,
keeping us apart.

Our tattered hearts,
weighed down by
the burden of our heartbeats,

telling the stories of
what we were
And what we will
never be. .

7. The Weight of Whys

Unanswered things are like poison,
Seeping slowly,
Eating away at the quiet corners of your mind.
Each day, a little more gone,
A little more heavy.

They give you anxiety
That shows up in still moments,
When you're alone with your thoughts.
They tease you with hope,
Then snatch it away,
Leaving you emptier than before.

You begin to wonder—
Why are people so selfish now?
Why is silence the easiest answer?
Why does caring feel like a weakness?
And why, oh why,
Do the goodbyes never come with explanations?

Some days, you scream inside.
Other days, you quietly ache.
But the weight of the unanswered
Stays the same.

And the "why"
Still lingers.

8. Your Eyes

Your eyes are the ocean
you wants to drown into,
It's just like a painting
of a story
that lies within
your soul,
screaming its purity
to the world
that has stopped
believing
in magic.

Your eyes are the truth
when everything is a lie
telling stories of
the dreams that died
and all the hopes
crushed,
they tell us how
people take a thing

of beauty
And turn it onto
a curse.

Your eyes now resembles the sky
which have consumed
the stars,
and now just
keeps shining
to lighten all
the dark shadows
of your future.

9. Moments

Far from my exasperations
Longingly I dream of you
sometimes with open,
sometimes with close eyes
nostalgic of the essence
of your presence
scrutinizing those
pure moments
whose memories
are now faded
with the tick of time
leaving only
footprints
behind.

10. Not All Who Wander...

Wandering, we find our way—
not by sitting still,
not by waiting like a stone
for someone else to lead us
to where we belong.

They say wandering means you're lost,
but how else do you learn
to listen to the noise,
to hear your own voice
through the chaos?

In getting lost,
we meet parts of ourselves
we never knew existed—
quiet dreams, buried truths,
the version of us we've been searching for.

To wander is not to drift.
It is to move with wonder,

to explore the unfamiliar
until it feels like home.

Because only through wandering
do we finally find
the real "you."

11. What the Mirror Knows

A mirror is a quiet canvas—
sometimes looking at you,
sometimes through you.
It shows beauty you forget,
flaws you try to hide,
and makes you pause—
is this really me?

Mirrors don't lie.
They reflect your truth—
your smile, your doubts,
your unspoken thoughts.
You can't hide from your own eyes,
not when they're staring back,
honest and still.

They show what others see,
but only you
know what it means.

12. The Comfort of Strangers

We search for strangers
To talk, to confess,
To pour out the thoughts we hide
Behind familiar smiles.

It's not that we don't love
Our friends, our family—
But they know us too well.
They see through the cracks.

They sense the tremble in our voice,
The shift in our eyes
When we say, "I'm fine."
And maybe that's what scares us.

Because with strangers,
We can wear new masks—
Or drop them completely,
Without fear of being known too deeply.

It's easier, somehow,
To open up to someone
Who holds no past of us,
And expects nothing more.

A passing moment of truth
With no lasting consequence—
Just a sliver of honesty
In a world where we keep pretending..

13. Prayers to the Moon

We have become
quiet, sad stories
told in silence,
written between the pauses
of our own voices.

We walk through days
with smiles that don't reach our eyes,
carrying loneliness
like a secret
we're too tired to hide.

There are nights
when the weight becomes too much —
and on those nights,
we whisper our hearts
to the moon.

We pray
not for grand things,

but for something soft,
something that stays.

We ask this moon —
the silent witness in the sky,
the keeper of light
in our darkest hours —

to send us a kind of love
that doesn't vanish
at the first sign of fear,
a love that burns,
not like fire that devours,
but like a flame that warms.

A love
that knows how to last.

A love
That doesn't fizzle,
doesn't fade,

Just stays.
Even when we forget
how to ask it to.

14. Hope

Hope
sometimes a blessing
written in between the
lines of our hands,
sometimes a curse
dangling from our thoughts
making us believe
the impossible.

But still,
we hold onto it—
like a flicker in the dark,
a voice that says
"maybe tomorrow,"
even when today
feels too difficult
to carry.

15. Tomorrow

We all hope for a better tomorrow,
Run through our dreams
Without pause or break.
Even when we fall and get hurt,
There's still a quiet hope inside
That tomorrow might be softer
Than today.

Tomorrow holds the promise—
A silver lining just beyond the clouds.
Like the farmer waits for rain,
Like the sky waits to clear after the storm,
Like the tree that sheds its old leaves
So the new ones can begin again.

Tomorrow is not some faraway land,
It's closer than we think—
Only one brave step away.
But that step must be taken,
So that your dreams don't slip

Out of reach.

Yesterday may have been heavy,
Today might feel heavier still.
But hold on—
Tomorrow could be the beginning
Of something better.

16. The Place We Seek

There is a hunger
for a place—
not made of bricks or walls,
but of warmth,
where nothing feels too broken
to mend.

A place where
being misunderstood
is rare,
and even when pain walks in,
healing follows closely behind,
hand in hand.

A place where
people make mistakes,
but apologies are not foreign.
Where the heart knows
that forgiveness
can grow even in the hardest soil.

A space where the universe
returns what it takes—
sometimes in different shapes,
but always in balance.
Where even the smallest joys
are seen as signs of magic.

Where no one hides
behind masks,
and love comes
not from perfection,
but from truth.

That is the place
we are all hungry for—
the one our hearts
secretly remember
and endlessly seek.

17. My Words

My words.
They just don't stay.
They vanish—
like smoke in the wind,
sometimes tangled in my thoughts,
other times lost in silly dreams
that drift like clouds above my head.

They disappear
into pages of books I read,
or maybe in the places I go—
maybe I leave them behind,
along with little pieces of myself.

I try to catch them,
piece by piece,
but they slip...
little by little.
You know how my hands always sweat?
Clammy palms,

never made for holding on—
not to words,
not to anything,
it seems.

Maybe they escape
into the cold night air,
whispering away
into the mystery of night,
Taken gently by the moon
who understands silence too well.

Still,
they don't come back to me.
As if they know—
if they do,
I'll weave them into poems
and hand them to people
who say they understand.
And I'll wonder...

Did they really get it?
Or did they just read it like any other poem—
not knowing
each word was squeezed
from the depths of me,
from the wild corners of my mind,

from the quiet hunger
of my creative soul?

30

18. Scars

Scars are hope.
They remind us we made it through—
through the pain,
the breaking,
the silence that followed.

They are marks of survival,
of battles we didn't think we'd win,
but somehow did.
Quietly, slowly,
but surely.

Scars are the cracks
where light finds its way in.
They don't dim us—
they define us.
They show where we've been
and how far we've come.

Scars are courage.

Not loud, not always seen—
but real.
The kind of courage
that shows up every day,
even when it's hard.

They are the proof
that we've felt deeply,
lost greatly,
and still chosen
to keep going.

They are the strength
that holds us together
when we feel like falling apart.
The quiet voice that says,
"you've done this before,
you can do it again."

So don't hide them.
Don't hate them.
Touch them.
Remember them.

Because your scars
are not the end of your story—

they're the reason
you're still writing it.

33

19. White

White.

The one we call pure,
the one we trust too easily,
the one we think is safe.

White —
the colour of untouched paper,
of first snow,
of promises whispered in innocence.

But white is not empty.
It holds everything —
every stain, every scar,
every trace of life
that touches it.

One touch,
one careless moment,
and it changes.

You can scrub it,
you can wash it,
you can try to make it new again —
but it always remembers.

White is high maintenance.
Fragile.
Demanding.

It fools you into thinking it's simple,
while hiding a thousand faces underneath.

The smiles we fake.
The truths we bury.
The fears we fold neatly out of sight.

Sometimes,
white feels like silence.
Too loud to ignore,
too delicate to break.

And at the very end —
when life lets go of its colours,
when the mind stops reaching —
there it is again.

White.

Not as an ending,
but as a beginning.

A blank space,
waiting for a new story.

A quiet canvas,
ready for whatever comes next.

A reminder —
that even after everything,
there is always the chance
to begin again.

20. Burning Quietly

We always see the moon,
lonely in the night.
But what if the sun feels the same?

It rises,
it sets,
never asking for rest.

We never stop to think,
does it want to hide?
To disappear,
to not give?

It burns,
it gives,
it never asks.

Maybe the sun is tired too,
but it stays.

Because we need it,
even when it wants to leave.

Maybe the sun is like us—
giving everything,
and asking for nothing.

But still, it stays.
And in that,
it keeps going.

21. When Art Finds You

When this logical world
pulls you under —
with its rules,
its straight lines,
its expectations that leave no room to feel —

Art finds you.
And saves you.

It could be a painting,
bursting with colors
you never knew lived inside you,
mirroring the chaos
you tried so hard to hide.

It could be a line from a poem,
soft yet sharp,
that touches something so deep,
you wonder if someone
has been listening

to the thoughts you never spoke aloud.

Sometimes,
it's a song.
The one that plays on repeat,
because your heart hasn't let go
of how it made you feel.

You sit in silence,
but your emotions
are screaming
through every lyric.

Art doesn't ask questions.
It doesn't expect answers.
It just holds space —
for everything you're too tired to explain.

In a world that demands logic,
art is the quiet reminder
that lets you believe in magic.

www.ingramcontent.com/pod-product-compliance
Lightning Source LLC
LaVergne TN
LVHW051236200726
843510LV00011B/1586